ANNOTATIONS

ON THE

SACRED WRITINGS OF THE HINDUS

BEING AN EPITOME
OF SOME OF THE MOST REMARKABLE AND LEADING
TENETS IN THE FAITH OF THAT PEOPLE

Illustrating their Priapic Rites and Phallic Principles

ANNOTATIONS

ON THE

SACRED WRITINGS OF THE HINDUS

BEING AN EPITOME OF SOME OF THE MOST REMARKABLE AND LEADING TENETS IN THE FAITH OF THAT PEOPLE

Illustrating their Priapic Rites and Phallic Principles

By

EDWARD SELLON,

Author of "The Monolitihic Temples of India," etc., etc.,
and Editor of an English Translation of the "Gita-Radhica-Krishna," a Sanskrit Poem.

New Edition.

GYAN

Published by

GYAN

Gyan Publishing House
5, Ansari Road
Daryaganj, New Delhi-110002
Phone: 011-47034999, 9811692060
E-mail: books@gyanbooks.com

Distribution Network
gyanbooks.com
India, USA, Canada, UK, Australia, France

ISBN : 978-81-212-2461-1 (PB)
First Published, 1902

2nd Impression 2021

Printed at: Gyan Press, Delhi.

Annotations
on the
Sacred Writings of the Hindus
Author: Edward Sellon

ANNOTATIONS

ON THE

SACRED WRITINGS OF THE HINDÜS

BEING AN EPITOME

OF SOME OF THE MOST REMARKABLE AND LEADING TENETS IN THE FAITH OF THAT PEOPLE

Illustrating their Priapic Rites and Phallic Principles

BY

EDWARD SELLON,

Author of "The Monolithic Temples of India," etc., etc., and Editor of an English translation of the "Gita-Radhica-Krishna," a Sanskrit Poem.

New Edition.

LONDON:

1902.

INTRODUCTION.

It has been suggested to the Author of the following pages, to compile a small treatise, which, without professing to be an abridgment of the Hindü Sacred Writings, should convey in a concise form an Epitome of the information that has been obtained with respect to the leading dogmas of the Brahminical Superstition.

When we reflect upon certain peculiarities of the Religious Worship practised by the Hindüs; on its great antiquity, on the fact, that two thousand years before the Christian æra it was, as at the present day, in full force; that it witnessed the rise, decline and fall of the Idolatry of Egypt, and of the great Western Mythology of Greece and Rome; that hitherto it has scarcely yielded in the slightest degree to the adverse influence of the Mohammedan race on the one hand, or to European dictation on the other; and that it exercises, by its system of caste, a powerful control over the manners, customs, costume and social status of the entire Hindū community, it becomes a subject fraught with interest to every cultivated mind, and offers an affecting but curious example of the power of a hoary and terrible superstition in degrading and enslaving so large a portion of the human race.

The sources from whence much of the material in this compilation are derived, are acknowledged in numerous notes.

It does not come within the compass of this sketch to enumerate all the theological dogmas contained in the Sacred Writings of the Hindūs; those only have been selected for annotation and remark which seem to have the most direct bearing on the object in view, in the elucidation of the worship of POWER—the Gnosticism of India.

ANNOTATIONS

ON THE

SACRED WRITINGS OF THE HINDÜS.

THE origin of the Religious Worship of the Hindüs is lost in remote antiquity. For many ages anterior to the time of *Menu*, their first Lawgiver, all that has been handed down to us by oral tradition seems to confirm the hypothesis, that they were worshippers of one God only, whom they designated *Brühm Atma*, "the Breathing Soul:" a spiritual Supreme Being, coeval with the formation of the world, without end, everlasting, permeating all space, the beneficent disposer of events. The worship of the Hindüs at this period was probably simple, and their ceremonies few. In process of time, however, the date of which cannot be correctly determined, they appear to have adopted a material type or emblem of *Brühm*: a rude block of stone began to be set up: this was the *Phallus*, or, as they termed it, the LINGA. This emblem had reference to the procreative Power seen throughout nature, and in that primæval age was regarded with the greatest awe and veneration. To the influence of this image was attributed the fructifying warmth which brought to perfection the fruits of the earth and contributed to the reproduction both of man, animals, and everything that has life.

This simple and primitive Idolatry came, by degrees, to diverge into the adoration of the elements, particularly Fire; and at length developed itself by the institution of an emanation from *Brühm Atma* in his Triune capacity; as Creator, Preserver or Saviour, and Destroyer. These attributes were deified under the names of *Brahma*, *Vishnu* and *Siva*, on whom were conferred three *Gunas* or qualities, viz., *Rajas* (passion), *Sat* (purity), and *Tumas* (darkness). This is the *Trimurti*.*

The next step towards the formation of a Pantheon was the institution of *Avatas* and *Avantaras*, *i.e.*, greater and lesser Incarnations; by which one or other of the *Triad* imparted a portion of his divine essence both to men (generally Bahurdurs or heroes) and to brutes. The tendency to deify heroes,

* "*Trimurti*, 'three formed,' *Murti* signifying also an Image. Our vital souls are, according to the *Védanta*, no more than images or *eidola* of the Supreme Spirit."—As. Res., vol. iii.

and irrational creatures, was not peculiar, however, to the Hindüs, for the Assyrians, Etruscans, Greeks and Romans had the same custom, as had also the Egyptians in a much more extended degree.

This system of *Avatas* was followed by an almost universal deification, not only of the elements and the heavenly bodies, but of every recognised attribute of the Supreme Being, and the Evil Spirit; Omnipotence, Beneficence, Virtue, Love, Vice, Anger, Murder; all receive a tangible form, until at the present time the Hindü Pantheon contains little short of a Million Gods and Demi-gods. It is admitted, however, that to many of these they pay only relative honour.

It is a little remarkable that of this host of Divinities, especially in Bengal, *Siva* is the God whom they are especially delighted to honour. As the Destroyer, and one who revels in cruelty and bloodshed this terrible deity, who has not inaptly been compared to the Moloch of Scripture, of all their Divinities suggests most our idea of the Devil. It may therefore be concluded that the most exalted notion of worship among the Hindüs is a service of *Fear*. The *Brahmins* say that the other Gods are good and benevolent, and will not hurt their creatures, but that *Siva* is powerful and cruel, and that it is necessary to *appease him.*

Although this deity is sometimes represented in the human form in his images, it is not thus that he is most frequently adored. The most popular representation of him is unquestionably the *Linga;* a smooth stone rising out of another stone of finer texture, *simulacrum membri virilis, et pudendum Muliebre.* This emblem is identical with *Siva* in his capacity of "Lord of all."

It is necessary, however, to observe here, that Professor Wilson, while admitting that "the *Linga* is perhaps the most ancient object of homage adopted in India," adds, *subsequently to the ritual of the Vedhas,* which was chiefly, if not wholly, addressed to the Elements, and particularly to fire. How far the worship of the *Linga* is authorised by the Vedhas is doubtful, but that it is the main purport of several of the *Puranas** there can be no doubt." †

The universality of *Linga puja* (or worship) at the period of the Mohammedan invasion of India is well attested. The Idol destroyed by Mahoud of Ghizni, notwithstanding the

---

* *Puranas*, the Modern Scriptures of the Hindüs, as distinguished from the Vedhas or more Ancient Scriptures.

† Wilson on Hindüs Sects.—As. Res., vol. xvii.

remarkable stories related by the Mohammedan chroniclers of a colossal image of human form which the Brahmins offered immense sums to save from destruction, but which upon being shattered by a blow from Mahoud's mace disgorged a vast treasure of gold and precious stones of inestimable value,—and the whole of which story Wilson proves is a pure fiction,—was nothing more than one of those mystical blocks of stone called Lingas.*

The worship of Siva under the type of the *Linga* is almost the only form in which that deity is reverenced. Its prevalence throughout the whole tract of the Ganges as far as Benares, is sufficiently conspicuous. In Bengal the *Lingam* Temples are commonly erected in a range of six, eight, or twelve on each side of a Ghaut† leading to the river. At Kalma is a circular group of one hundred and eight temples erected by the Rajah of Burdwan. These temples, and indeed all those found in

---

* As. Res., vol. xvii., pp. 208, 209 and 210.

† *Ghaut*, "a high place," applied to a pass, such as the *Laulpet* pass, where the traveller ascends from the campaign country to the table-land of the *Deccan:* also, and in this instance, signifying an artificial "high place," constructed either of stone or marble, with an immense flight of steps leading down to the river. There are numerous *Ghauts*, or *Ghâts*, of this description on the banks of the Ganges, where the banks are too high to allow the people to approach the stream with safety.

Bengal, consist of a simple chamber of a square form surmounted by a pyramidal centre; the area of each is very small. The Linga of black or white marble, and sometimes of alabaster slightly tinted and gilt, is placed in the middle.

Speaking of *Siva* and Pawáti, M. de Langle says, "Les deux divinités dont il s'agit, sont très souvent et très pieusement adorées, sous la figure du Linga (le Phallus des anciens) et de l'yoni, dans leur mystérieuse conjonction. L'yoni se nomme aussi *Bhaga* (pudendum muliebre), *Madheri* douce, et *Argha*, vase en forme de batéau, dans lequel on offre des fleurs à la divinité, tels sont les noms de *l'Adhera-Sacti* (energie de la conception vivifiée par le Linga). Quand cette déesse est representée par le symbole que je viens d'indiquer, elle prend le nom de *Devi* (divine) plus communément que ceux de *Bhavani*, de *Pracritri*, &c. Suivant les théologians Hindous, une vive discussion s'éleva entre *Pavati* (née des montagnes) et *Maha-deva* (le grand dieu), peu de temps après leur mariage, sur l'influence des sexes dans la production des êtres; ils convinrent de créer séparément une race d'individus. Les enfants de Mahadeva furent nombreux, et se dévouèrent au culte de le divinité mâle; mais il manquoient d'intelligence et de force, et ils étoient mal conformés, ceux de Parvati étoient beâux, bien faits et d'un excellent naturel; cependant, obsédés par les *Lingadja*, ou enfants de *Maha-deva*, ils envinrent aux mains avec eux, et les vainquirent. Mahadeva alloit dans sa fureur anéantir d'un coup-d'œil les Yônîdja vainqueurs si Parvati ne l'eut appaisé. Les Brâhmanes offrent aux Linga des fleurs, et ont soin quand ils font leurs cérémonies d'allumer sept lamps,* lesquelles, selon Mathurin, vessière de la croze, ressemblent au chandelier à sept branches des Juifs, qu'on voit à Rome sur l'arc Titus. Les femmes portent des Lingas au cou et aux bras; celles qui desirent devenir fécondés rendent à cette idole un culte tout particulier; elles ont il d'autant plus de confiance dans ses prêtres que ceux-ci font vœu de chasteté."†

The offerings are presented at the threshold.

Benares, however, is the peculiar seat of this form of worship. The principal Deity, Siva, there called *Viweswarra*, as observed already, is a Linga; and most of the chief objects of pilgrimage are similar blocks of stone. No less than forty-seven Lingas are visited, all of pre-

---

* De Langle is in error here. The Punchaty, as its name implies, consists of five, not seven lamps.

† Monuments Anciens et Moderns de l'Hindoustan.—Par L. L. de Langle; Paris, 2 vols, folio, 1810.

eminent sanctity; but there are hundreds of inferior note still worshipped, and thousands whose fame and fashion have passed away. It is a singular fact, that upon this adoration of the procreative and sexual Sacti (or power) seen throughout nature, hinges the whole gist of the Hindü faith, and notwithstanding all that has been said by half-informed persons to the contrary, this puja does not appear to be prejudicial to the morals of the people. "Among a people of such exuberant fancy as the Hindüs," says Sir William Jones, "it is natural that everything should receive form and life. It is remarkable to what a degree their works of imagination are pervaded by the idea of sexuality. Indeed, it seems never to have entered into the heads of the Hindü Legislators and people that anything natural could be offensively obscene, a singularity which pervades all their writings, but is no proof of the depravity of their morals, thence the worship of the *Linga* by the followers of *Siva*, and of the Yoni by the followers of *Vishnu*." *

We find amongst the sacred paintings of the Hindüs numerous representations of devotees, both male and female, adoring the *Linga*,

* Sir W. Jones's Works, vol. ii., p. 311.

"It is unattended in Upper India by any indecent or indelicate ceremonies."—Wilson on Hindü Sects. As. Res., vol. xvii.

and a description of one of these pictures will suffice for them all. The domestic temple, in which the emblem is usually placed, is a *Dewal*, a term derived from *Deva*, a deity, and *Havela*, a house, *i.e.*, the "house of God." Indeed, the natives have no such word as "Pagoda" for their temples, which are always called *Dewals*.

The worshipper is seated, dressed, and arrayed in all her jewels, as directed by the Ritual. In her right hand she holds a *Mala*, or Rosary of one hundred and eight round beads, which is not visible, as her hand is placed within a bag of gold brocade *(Kampkab)* called *Gumuki*, to keep off insects or any adverse influence. Her *langi* or bodice is yellow, her dress transparent muslin edged with gold *(upervastra)*. In front of her are the five lamps, called panchaty, used in this *Puja*, viz., *Jari*, or spouted vessel for lustral water; the *Dippa*, or Cup, to sprinkle the flowers which she has offered, and which are seen on the *Linga*; and, lastly, the *Gantha*, or sacred bell, used frequently during the recapitulation of the prescribed *Muntrus*, or incantations. Nearly all the *Pujas* are conducted with the frequent ringing of bells, and the object of this is twofold—first to wake up the attention at particular parts of the service; and secondly, to scare away malignant *Dewtas* and evil spirits; precisely, in fact, for the same reasons as they are used at the celebration of Mass in Roman Catholic countries.

The Linga and the Earth are, according to the Hindüs, identical, and the mountain of Meru is termed the "Navel of the Earth." Meru is supposed to be the centre of the universe, and is said to be 8,400 *yojans* high, 32,000 broad at the top, 16,000 at the bottom. It is circular, and formed like an inverted cone. This notion was not confined to India, for when Cleanthes asserted that the earth was in the shape of a cone,* this is to be understood only of this mountain, the *Meru* of India. Anaximenes† said that this column was plain and of stone, exactly like *Meru-pargwette (Pawati)* of the inhabitants of Ceylon.‡ "This mountain," says he, "is entirely of stone, 68,000 yojanas high, and 10,000 in circumference, and of the same size from the top to the bottom."

In India the followers of Buddha§ insist that this mountain is like a drum, with a swell in the middle, in the same form in fact as the *Tomtoms* used in the East. In the

* As. Res., viii.

† Plutarch de placit. philosoph.

‡ Joinville As. Res., vol. vii.

§ Trailoyoya-Derpana.

west, formerly, the same opinion had been expressed by Lucippus, and the *Buddhists* in India give that shape also to islands. This figure is given as an emblem of the re-union of the powers of nature. *Meru* is the sacred and primeval *Linga:* and the earth beneath is the mysterious *Yoni* expanded, and open like the *Padma* or Lotus. The convexity in the centre is the navel of *Vishnu,* and the physiological mysteries of their religion is often represented by the emblem of the Lotus ; where the whole flower signifies both the earth and the two principles of its fecundation. The germ is both *Meru* and the *Linga;* the petals and filaments are the mountains which encircle *Meru,* and are also the type of the *Yoni.* The four leaves of the Calyx are the four vast regions turning towards the four cardinal points. According to the two geographical systems of the Hindüs, the first or more ancient is (as set forth in the *Puran*) the Earth described as a convex surface gradually sloping towards the borders, and surrounded by the ocean. The second, and more modern system, is that adopted by their astronomers. The followers of the *Puranas* consider the Earth as a *flat surface,* or nearly so, their knowledge does not extend much beyond the old continent, or the superior hemisphere ;

but astronomers being acquainted with the globular shape of the earth, and of course with an inferior hemisphere, were under the necessity of borrowing largely from the superior part in order to fill up the inferior one.

The leaves of the Lotus represent the different islands in the ocean around *Jambu*, and according to the Hindü system, the whole earth floats upon the waters like a boat. The *Argha** of the Hindüs and the Cymbium of the Egyptians are also emblems of the earth

---

* The three words *Amba*, *Nabbi* and *Argha* seemed to have caused great confusion among the Greek mythologists, who even ascribe to the earth all the fanciful shapes of the Argha, which was intended at first as a mere emblem. Hence they represented it in the form of a boat, of a cup, or of a quoit with a boss in the centre, sloping towards the circumference, where they placed the ocean.—Agathem. book i. c. 1.

Others described the earth as a square or parallelogram, and Greece was supposed to lie on the summit, with Delphi in the navel, or central part of the whole.—Pind. Pyth., 6. Eurip. Ion., v., 233.

While the Jews, and even the early Christians, insisted that the true navel of the earth was Jerusalem, and the Mohammedans, Mecca.

The Argha is a type of the *A'dhara-Sacti*, or Power of Conception, exerted and vivified by the Linga or Phallus, one and the same with the ship Argo, which was built, according to Orpheus, by Juno and Pallas, and according to Apollonius, by Pallas and Argos, at the instance of Juno.—Orph. Argon., v., 66, Apoll., lib. ii., 5, 1190. As. Res., vol. iii.

and of the *Yoni.* The *Argha*, or Cymbium, signifies a vessel, cup or dish, in which fruits or flowers are offered to the deities, and ought to be in the shape of a boat; though many are oval, circular, or even square.

Iswarra, or Bacchus, is styled *Argha-Nautha*, or "Lord of the boat-shaped vessel"; and *Osiris* the *Iswara*, or Bacchus of Egypt, according to Plutarch, was commander of the *Argo*, and was represented by the Egyptians in a boat carried on the shoulders of a great many men. The ship worshipped by the *Suevi*, according to Tacitus, was the *Argha*, or *Argo*, and the type of the *pudendum muliebre.* "The Agha, or Yoni, with the *Linga* of stone, is found all over India as an object of worship. Flowers are offered to it, and the water, which is poured on the *Linga*, runs into the rim, which represents the *Yoni*, and also the *fossa navicularis*, and instead of the *Linga*, *Iswarra* is sometimes represented standing in the middle, as Osiris in Egypt."*

Plutarch has said of the Egyptians, that they had inserted nothing into their worship without a reason, nothing merely fabulous, nothing superstitious, as many suppose, but their institutions have either a reference to morals or something useful in life. The

* As. Res., viii.

mass of mankind lost sight, however, of morality in the multiplicity of rites, as it is easier to practise ceremonies than to subdue passions; so it was in India and Egypt.

In the course of investigating the ceremonies of the Hindūs, and in attempting to elucidate their meaning, it will be found necessary to draw an analogy between them and those of the Egyptians. The resemblance is very striking, they mutually serve to explain each other. When the Sepoys, who accompanied Lord Hutchinson in his Egyptian expedition, saw the temple at Hadja Silsili they were very indignant with the natives of the place for allowing it to fall into decay, conceiving it to be the temple of their own god, Siva, a fact, to say the least of it, no less singular than interesting.

The annihilation of the sect and worship of *Brahma*, as the Iswarra or "Supreme Lord," is described at large in the *Kasi-chandra* of the *Scanda Puran*, where the three powers are mentioned as contending for precedence. *Vishnu* at last acknowledges the superiority of Siva, but *Brahma*, on account of his presumptuous obstinacy, had one of his heads cut off by Siva, and his puja, or worship, abolished.

The intent of this legend is evidently to advance the claims of the *Saiva* sect, and if we substitute the contending facts for the battle of the Deutas, or angels, the fable will appear not quite destitute in historical fact, nor wholly without foundation.

The contention of schismatics from the same stock is always more inveterate than where the difference is total. The sect of *Brahma* claimed exclusive pre-eminence for the object of their choice as being the Creative Power, the *Iswarra*, or "Supreme Lord." The two other sects joined against the followers of *Brahma*. The sect of Siva, being the most powerful, rendered theirs the established religion, and claimed for *Siva*, in his turn, the exclusive title of *Iswarra*. The sect of *Vishnu* or *Heri* at length emerged from its obscurity, and in concert with the adorers of *Sacti* (or the female power), destroyed and abolished the sect and worship of *Siva*, and then *Vishnu, Heri*, (or *Krishna*) became the Iswarra, or "Supreme Lord," and his worship became the established religion. This appears to have been the case in Egypt; and notwithstanding that all affinity between the two systems has of late years been so strongly denied, if we substitute Osiris for Brahma, Horus for Vishnu, Typhon for Siva, and Isis for the Sacti (or female power), the narrative agrees in every respect.

Again, the Sun is one of the forms of *Vishnu* (as *Heri*); Osiris and *Horus* are both said to have been identical with the Sun. The bull of *Siva* *(Nandi)* is the same as the bulls Apis and Mnevis of Memphis and Thebes.

He (*Nandi*) is the *Vahan*, or vehicle of this divinity: the Bull is the type of justice, whose body is *Parameswarra*, and whose every joint is virtue; whose three horns are the three *Vedhs*, and whose tail ends where *Aa'herma*, or injustice, begins. The Phallus of Osiris* was an object of worship, and is also the emblem of Siva.

Bacchus or Osiris was represented by an equilateral triangle, and the sectarian mark of the worshippers of Siva is this hieroglyphic. The worship of Bacchus was the same as that which is paid to Siva, it had the same obscenities, the same cruel,

---

* "Now that Osiris is none other in reality than the great principle of fecundity is further evident from their manner of celebrating the Pramylia (a festival which has been before observed to bear a resemblance to the *Priapeia* of the Greeks), in which they carry about in procession and expose to public view a statue of the God with a *triple-phallus*, signifying hereby that he is a first principle, and that every such principle, by means of its generative faculty, multiplies what proceeds from or is produced by it."—Plutar. de Iside et Osirides, xxxvi.

bloodthirsty rites, and the same emblem of the generative power.

The Hindü sacrifices to *Durga*, or *Kali*, are a striking exemplification of this hypothesis. Mr. Patterson informs us that "When the stroke is given which severs the head of the victim from its body, the cymbals strike up, the tumtums beat, the kranch, or buccinum, is blown, and the whole assembly, shouting, smear- their faces with the blood; they roll themselves in it, and, dancing like demons, accompany their dances with obscene songs, allusions and gestures." *

The Abbé Pluche mentions the same particulars of the assistants in the sacrifices of Dyonisius or Bacchus.

Durga, *Káli*, or *Maha Káli* as the *Sacti*, spouse or energetic will of *Siva*, the destructive power, bears a remarkable analogy with the Moloch of Scripture, as well as with Typhon, Saturn, Dis, Pluto, and other divinities of the West. She is eternity, and under this attribute is often represented as trampling her lord *Siva* under foot; sometimes in paintings we see her sitting upon him in the act of *coitus*, by which we are to understand that his worship will only last to the end of the world, and then to pass

---

* As. Res., vol. viii.

away for ever. She is represented *in coitu* as typical of the creative power of *Siva* during the period of his administration, she being the medium, or Sacti, by which his will is carried into operation.

*Maha Kali** delights in bloodshed and cruelty, and human sacrifices are very acceptable to her. In images and paintings she is pourtrayed as holding in her four hands the heads of victims streaming with blood. Over her shoulders is thrown a necklace of human skulls. She is seated on the sacred *Padma*, or Lotus, and wears a golden tiara on her head. Other representations there are of this terrible divinity, in which her features are distorted, hideous fangs project from her mouth; her fingers are armed with talons, like a bird of prey, while her body is entwined with serpents. To Maha Kali is attributed pestilence, rapine, lust, murder, and all the ills of humanity. She is the protectress of murderers, thieves, prostitutes, panders, and all evil doers. Under the name of *Bowani* she is the special patroness of the *Thugs*.† The buffalo is sacrificed to her in the absence of a human victim, while the

---

* *Bhayánana*, one of the names of this Goddess, is the same as Phœbe.

† Thugs: Robbers who always strangle their victims previous to plundering them.

Brahminee bull and cow are held in the utmost veneration.

When the attributes of the Supreme Being began to be viewed in the light of distinct individuals, mankind attached themselves to the worship of the one or the other exclusively, and arranged themselves into sects: the worshippers of *Siva* introduced the doctrine of the eternity of matter. In order to reconcile the apparent contradiction of assigning the attribute of creation to the principle of Destruction, they asserted that the dissolution and destruction of bodies was not real with respect to matter, which was in itself indestructible, although its modifications were in a constant succession of mutation; that the power must necessarily unite in itself the attributes of creation and apparent destruction; that this power and matter are two distinct and co-existent principles in nature; the one active, the other passive; the one male, the other female; and that creation was the effect of the mysterious union of the two.

This Union is worshipped under a variety of names: *Bhava*, *Bhavani*, *Mahadeva*, *Mahamaya*, &c. Thus the attribute of creation was usurped from *Brahma*, by the followers of Siva, to adorn and characterise their favourite divinity.

This seems to have been a popular worship for a great length of time, out of which sprang two sects: the one personified the whole Universe and dispensations of providence (in the regulation of it) under the name of *Prakriti*, and which we from the Latin call nature. This sect retains the *Sacti* only, and were the originators of the *Sactas* sects, or worshippers of POWER, before and hereafter to be alluded to. The other sect took for their symbol the Male emblem (*Linga*) unconnected with the female *Sacti* (or *Yoni*). There was also a third sect, who adored both male and female.

According to Theodoret, Arnobius, and Clemens of Alexandria, the *Yoni* of the Hindüs was the sole object of veneration in the mysteries of Eleusis.* When the people of Syracuse were sacrificing to goddesses, they offered cakes in a certain form, called *mulloi*;† and in some temples, where the priestesses were probably ventriloquists, they so far imposed on the credulous multitude who came to adore the *Vulva*, as to make them believe that it spoke and gave oracles. The Phallic rites were so well-known among the Greeks that a metre consisting of

---

* Demosthenes of the Crown.

† Apuleius, p. 802.

three torches only derived its name therefrom.

In the opinion of those who compiled the Puranas, Phallus was first publicly worshipped by the name of *Básewarra-Linga* on the banks of the *Cumudoati*, or Euphrates; and the Jews, according to Rabbi Aeha, seem to have had some such idea, as may be collected from what is said regarding the different earths which formed the body of Adam.*

---

* Gemara Sanhedrim, c. 30, cited by Ryland.

If reference be made to chap. iv., vol. iii., of Lewis's Origines Hebrææ, much curious information will be found regarding the "Idolatry of the Hebrews," which not only plainly shows that they adored Phallus, but goes far to confirm the hypothesis that the object of veneration in the Ark of the Covenant was the emblem itself, or a type of it.

At p. 23, vol. iii., we read that "The most ancient monuments of Idolatry among the Gentiles, were consecrated *Pillars* (Lingas?) or Columns, which the Hebrews were forbidden to erect as objects of divine homage and adoration." Yet he adds, "This practice is conceived to arise from an *imitation of Jacob*, who took a stone and *set it up*," &c. Again, "This stone was held in great veneration in future times by the Jews and removed to *Jerusalem*." They were accustomed "to *anoint this stone*, and from the word *Bethel*, the place where the pillar was erected, came the word Bætylia among the Heathen, which signified rude stones which they worshipped, either as *symbols* of *Divinity*, or as *true gods* animated by some heavenly power." Indeed, it would seem not improbable that the erection of the *Pillar of Jacob* actually gave rise to the worship of Phallus among some of the Pagan peoples. "For," says Lewis, "the

The extraordinary analogy between the Sacti and Eleusinian mysteries is very striking. There is a Greek Vase in the Hamiltonian Collection at the British Museum, which represents the purification of a woman who is a candidate for the office of Sacti

---

learned *Bochart* asserts that the Phœnicians (at least as the Jews think) first worshipped *this very stone* which *Jacob anointed*, and afterwards consecrated others," &c.

It is to little purpose that we are reminded that the Jews were forbidden by their law to "make unto themselves any graven image," for, as Lewis shows in the following passage, there may be exceptions to this, as to every other general rule.

"Notwithstanding," he says, "the severity of the Law against the making of Images, yet, as Justin Martyr observes in his Book against Trypho, it must be somewhat mysterious, that God in the case of the *Brazen Serpent should command an image to be made*, for which, he says, one of the Jews confessed he never could hear a reason from any of their Doctors."

The brazen serpent continued to be worshipped by the Jews, and to have incense offered to that Idol, till the reign of Hezekiah:

"For it being written in the Law of Moses, '*whosoever* looks upon it shall live,' they fancied they might obtain blessings by its mediation, and therefore thought it worthy to be worshipped. Our learned Dr. Jackson observes, 'that the pious Hezekiah was moved with the greater indignation against the worship of this image, because *in truth it never was a type of our Saviour*, but *a figure of his grand enemy*,'" &c.

Then we find the Jews relapsing into Idolatry by the adoration of the golden calf, set up too, not by a few schismatics, but by the entire people, with Aaron at their head. The calf superstition was doubtless a relic of what

(to use an Indian word), she is about to be initiated into the greater mysteries. This woman is naked and stands near a font, in which her right hand is placed, her body has already been washed with some soapy substance, and scraped with the stirgil, which

---

they had seen in Egypt in the worship of Apis and Mnevis. Next we have the golden calves set up by Jeroboam at Dan and Bethel.

Then follows (Judges viii. 22, &c.) the worship of Gideon's Ephod.

"The *Ephod* made by Gideon with the spoil of the Midianites became *after his death* an object of Idolatry." —Ibid. p. 41.

We have also Micah's Images and *Teraphim.*

The Samaritan Temple upon Mount Gerizim. "The Jews accuse the Samaritans of two instances of Idolatry committed in this place: the first, that they worshipped the Image of a Dove; the other, that they paid divine adoration to certain Teraphims or Idol Gods that were hid under that mountain."—Ibid. p. 55.

We learn from St. Jerome (who received it by tradition from the ancient Jews, and indeed it is so stated in Numbers xxv. 1, 2, &c.; xxiii. 28, and numerous other passages of the Old Testament), that the Jews adored Baal Phegor (Baal Pheor), the Priapus of the Greeks and Romans. "It was," he says, "principally worshipped by women *colentibus maxime fœminis Baal Phegor, ob obscœni magnitudinem, quem nos Priapum possumus appellare.*"

"The Adoration," Maimonides observes, "made to this Idol called *Pehor*, consisted in discovering the mons veneris before it."

Chemosh (probably the same as Baal Pheor) also received the homage of the Jews, as also did Milcom, Molech, Baal berith (or Cybele), and numerous others.

From all this it will be seen that the Jews fell into

is seen near her feet. The priest who assists has a palm branch in his hand, which was sometimes of gold. He finishes the purification by an aspersion, and a prayer adapted to the ceremony.

The painting on another Vase in the same

Idolatry, and Phallic Idolatry too; consequently there will not appear anything so very startling in the supposition that the Ark of the Covenant contained a Phallus. We have seen that the *Stone* of Jacob was held in peculiar "*veneration*," was "*worshipped*" and "*anointed*;" we know from the Jewish records that the Ark was supposed to contain a table of *stone*, and if it can be demonstrated that that stone was phallic, and yet identical with the sacred name Jehovah, or Yehovah, which, written in unpointed Hebrew with four letters, is IEVE or IHVH (the HĘ being merely an aspirate and the same as E), this process leaves us the two letters I and V (or in another of its forms U). Then, if we add the I *in* the U, we have the "holy of holies," we also have the Linga and Yoni and Argha of the Hindüs, the Iswarra or "supreme lord," and here we have the whole secret of its mystic and arc-celestial import, confirmed in itself by being identical with the Linyoni of the Ark of the Covenant.

In Gregorie's Works,* pp. 120-21, is a passage to the effect that "*Noah daily prayed in the Ark before the Body of Adam*," *i.e.*, before the Phallus (Adam being the primitive Phallus, great Procreator of the human race).

"It may possibly seem strange," he says, "that this orison should be daily said before the body of *Adam*," but "it is a most confessed Tradition among the Eastern men that *Adam* was commanded by God that his dead body should be kept above ground till a fulness of time should

---

* Gregorie's "Notes and Observations upon several passages in Scripture."—Vol. i., 4to., Lond., 1684.

collection is thus described by D'Hancarville [vide Plate 29 of his Edit. of Greek and Etruscan Vases]—"La peinture de ce Vase blesse l'honnêtété et la pudeur, on y voit représentées deux Bacchantes toutes nues

---

come to commit it to the *middle of the earth** by a priest of the Most High God."

"This body of Adam was embalmed and transmitted from father to son, till at last it was delivered up by Lamech into the hands of Noah." Again, "The middle of the Ark was the place of prayer, and made holy by the presence of Adam's body."—Ibid. p. 121. "And so soon as ever the day began to break, Noah *stood up towards the body of Adam, &c., &c., and prayed.*"

To return, however, to the tables of stone, and to the *Pillar of Jacob.* Our modern notion of their form is a diagram, or in other words, two head-stones placed side by side. Now if we alter the positio n a little, allowing one to recline horizontally, surmounted by the other perpendicular, we shall obtain a complete Linga and Yoni, the "sacred Name" of the holy of holies before mentioned, and the *Pillar* or Mast in the Argha or boat as represented in the Ark of the Egyptians. The treatment of the Wings of the supporting doves, on each side of this ark, conveys to us a pretty correct idea of where the Hebrews obtained their Cherubim or Seraphim—only substituting a human head and body for the birds.

Upon consulting the Hebrew dictionary of Gesenius we shall find the word *aroun* and *aron* signifying an *ark*, a *chest.* In Genesis i. 26, the word is used as a mummy chest, or coffin, for Joseph in Egypt. The ark of the covenant might in the same way be called the Coffin.

For the above reasons it is concluded that the object of veneration in the Ark of the Covenant, of the Jews, was a Phallus.

---

* Mount Moriah—the Meru of India.

qui vout se laver *probablement avec du vin* pour oindre leur corps et auprès d'elles un Faune, or Siléne. Ces deux femmes par cette préparation et cette lustration prescrite par la loi se disposent peutêtre à assister aux mystères de Bacchus. Nous ne rapporterons pas ici les indécences lubriques que se commetorient dans ces brutaux mystères et qui avex fondement on été reprochées aux Gentils par les apologistes de la Religion Chrétienne."

It has already been remarked that the secret of the Eleusian Mysteries is supposed to have consisted in the adoration of the *Yoni;* and from the representations of the initiation, just cited, bearing a striking analogy to "the *Sri chakra,* the ring or full initiation," as prescribed by the *Tantra* referred to by Wilson, even to the washing of the body with *wine,* leaves but little doubt of their identity of the rites.

The probability that Isis was the Sacti (or POWER) of Egypt* has already been shown; and how far its adoration was known to the Assyrians is now to be considered.

---

*"Now *Universal Nature,* in its utmost and most perfect extent, may be considered as made up of these three things, of *Intelligence,* of *Matter,* and of that which is the result of both these, in the Greek language called *Kosmos*—the first of these is the same with what Plato is wont to call the *Idea,*

The numerous terra-cotta figures and images in ivory, to which Layard has given the general name of Venus (*Kún*), seem unquestionably to be an impersonation of *Sacti*, or the female power, as the *Yoni* is rather obtrusively represented in many of these statuettes, while the *fissure* and other natural appendages are absent in others. In the former not only is the yoni pourtrayed, but a certain ornament on the mons veneris is curled, precisely in the same conventional manner as is seen in the beards of the Male Statues in the Assyrian antiquities; while in the latter, the *true Venus*, the fissure and the appendages are omitted.

---

the *Father;* to the second of them he has given the name of the *Mother*, the Nurse, and the place and *Receptacle of generation;* and to the latter of them that of the offspring and the *Production*—so again with regard to the Egyptians, there is good reason to conclude that they were wont to liken this *Universal Nature* to what they called the most beautiful and perfect *Triangle;* the same as does Plato himself in that nuptial diagram, &c.—Now in this *Triangle*, which is rectangular, the perpendicular side is imagined equal to three, the base to four, and the hypothenuse, which is equal to the other two containing sides, to five. In this scheme, therefore, we must suppose that the Perpendicular is designed by them to represent the Masculine nature, the Base the Feminine, and that the Hypothenuse is to be looked upon as the offspring of both; and accordingly the *first* of them will aptly enough represent Osiris, or the prime cause; the second Isis, or the receptive power; the last, Orus, or the common effect of the other two."—*Plutarch de Iside et Osirides*, lvi.

One is therefore led to believe that the adoration of *Sacti* was a prominent feature in the Assyrian worship. And this idea is confirmed by a bas-relief of clay found at Susa, which gives a nude figure having the *yoni* depicted, and holding in her hands the *Argha.** The attitude of this figure, and the manner in which the Argha is placed in her hands, resembles in a remarkable manner the images of the Hindü goddess *Devi.*

Camala or *Laksmi* is the Hindü Venus, and generally draped. *Radha,* assumed to be an incarnation of *Laksmi* (but as the *Sacti* of *Krishna,* adored by the *Sactas* Sects of *Radhaballabhis*), is invariably nude, with the *Yoni* uncovered.

For representations of (what may be thought to be) the Assyrian *Sacti* (or impersonation of the female generative principle) the reader is referred to a collection of Images in the Assyrian department of the British Museum.

The *Linga* of the Assyrians was typified by a cone (or the Membrum Virile in its puerile form), numerous specimens of which were found projecting from the walls of the

---

* Originals in the British Museum.

Palace of Nimroud, of which examples may also be seen at the British Museum.

The Assyrians do not appear, however (like the Linyonijas of the Hindüs), to have worshipped the Sacti *in union*, as we find it taught in the Tantras,—at least no delineations of the male and female conjunction have been found *as objects of worship.*

Gorius, in his splendid work on Etruscan Antiquities, gives a plate of two phalli, bearing inscriptions, the form of which objects resemble in too remarkable a degree the Hindü Linga to be omitted here; but whether the square base from which these emblems rise is to be regarded as a yoni cannot readily be determined; but the Hindü Lingas are frequently (as at Elephanta, for example) mounted on a square base, the base being the Yoni.

Patterson has already been cited in confirmation of the assertion that the excitation of "obscene mirth" is a principal object in most of the Hindü Plays and Sacred Mysteries during the festival of Huli and the *Dusserah;* and the numerous libidines interspersed among the engravings of d'Hancarville's edition of the Hamiltonian Collection of Vases, prove that such was also the case in Greece and Etruria; but from the circumstance of Parrhasius being the first painter who delineated the representations called *libidines* in that part of the world, and from the pediments of many of the most antique cave temples of India, containing sculpture of this description, one is led to the conclusion that the practice arose in the East.

The clown and pantaloon of the modern carnival and our pantomimes are simply modified relics of antiquity : precisely similar characters are found depicted on vases of both Greek and Etruscan workmanship ; but to suit the taste of that age these actors to their grotesque masks and costumes added an enormous phallus of *red leather*,* which Suidas termed ithiphalli.

The scenes represented on the ancient stage are continued to the present day throughout the East.

The pediments of their temples, both ancient and modern, and their sacred cars are loaded with *libidines*, many of the combinations being of a most debasing character.

But it must be borne in mind that these representations, whether of the character of theatrical performances or in that of sculpture, were regarded by the ancients as a part of their religious system, as it is now accepted by the Hindūs of the present day.

---

* Ruber Porectus.—Hor.

How far the general character and moral tone of the Hindüs will bear comparison with the dwellers in the capitals of Europe is a point which may safely be left to the decision of those travellers who have had an opportunity of visiting and residing among both communities.*

Of the practices of the Ancients it is now more difficult to form an accurate judgment, nor is it easy to determine the precise period when, from the natural corruption of human nature, religious observances gradually merged into licentious practices. It is well known that the most able and eloquent writers of antiquity flourished exactly at that period when these innovations had crept in ; and that they were most eloquent in denouncing them. Modern notions of the state of the manners and customs of these times are mainly derived from those very denunciations, and such corruptions will always form an integral part of our nature.

We learn from the Vedhas, the most

---

* One of the most accomplished Oriental scholars of our times, to whom the public is indebted for a *Telugu* Dictionary, and a translation of the Bible into the same language, a resident for thirty years in India, has recorded his judgment that, on the questions of probity and morality, Europeans (notwithstanding their boasted Christianity and morality), as compared with the Hindüs, "*have not much to boast of*."

ancient and authoritative Scriptures of the Hindüs, that "in the beginning the Breathing Soul *(Brühm-Atma)* moved upon the face of the waters." "This world," says Menu, "was a chaos, undiscernible altogether, when the Supreme Being, manifesting himself in five elements and other glorious forms, perfectly dispelled the gloom." As water is thus represented as the vehicle of creation, and the Padma or Lotus is a water plant from which each god at his birth emerges, it will be seen why this aquatic weed is held to be so peculiarly sacred in the eyes of the Hindüs. The Lotus is also a symbol of reproduction and generation, the flower of concealment, night, silence, mystery, and regarded with nearly the same veneration as the Yoni itself. In the poetical language of the Hindüs the Padma, under its various appellations, is frequently alluded to, and is held in peculiar sanctity, not only in Hindustan, but in Thibet, Nepaul, Siam, China, Burmah, and Ceylon, where temples and the images of the gods are decked with it.

The Hindüs adore the Lotus for other reasons; for example, because being able to reproduce itself without the assistance of the male pollen, it is a type of the androgynous or hermaphroditic character of the Deity. For the same reason this plant was also held sacred by the Egyptian priests.

Payne Knight's* account of the Lotus is interesting. He says, "The lotus is the nelumbo of Linnæus. It grows in the water, and amongst its broad leaves puts forth a flower, in the centre of which is formed the seed vessel, shaped like a bell or inverted cone, punctuated in the top with little cavities or cells in which the seeds grow; the orifices of these cells being too small to let the seeds drop out when ripe, they shoot forth into new plants in the places where they were formed; the bulb of the vessel serving as a matrix to nourish them until they acquire such a degree of magnitude as to break it open and release themselves. After which, like other aquatic weeds, they take root wherever the current deposits them."

Twelve *Lingas* are particularly mentioned in the *Kedara Kalpa* of the *Nandi-upa-puran*, as being of peculiar sanctity. In this *Purán*, *Siva* is made to say, "I am omnipresent, but I am especially in twelve forms and places."

---

* A Dissertation on the Worship of Priapus, by R. Payne Knight, Lond., 1786.

These he enumerates as follows—

1—*Somanatha*, in *Samashtra*, i.e., *Surat.*

2—*Malikijuna*, or *Sri Sala.*

3—*Mahakala*, or *Ougein.*

4—*Om'kala.* Shrine of Mahadeo (or Great God, a name of *Siva*) at *Om'kala Mandatta.*

5—*Amareswarra*, in *Ujayai*, near the Hill.

6—*Vaidyanath*, at *Deoghur*, in Bengal. (This temple is still in existence, and a celebrated place of pilgrimage.)

7—*Ramása*, at *Sethubandha*, on the island of *Ramissaram*, between Ceylon and the Continent. (Here the *Linga* is fabled to have been set up by *Rama.*) This temple is still in tolerable repair, and one of the most magnificent in India, with a superb gateway one hundred feet in height.*

8—*Bhomasandkara*, in *Dakini*, which is in all probability the same as *Bhimeswarra*, a *Linga* worshipped at *Dracharam*, in the *Raja Mahendri* district, and there venerated as one of the chief of the twelve.

9—*Not known.*

10—*Tryambaka*, on the banks of the *Gomati (Goomtee?).*

11—*Gantamessa*—(site uncertain).

---

* For a print of it, *vide* "Monuments de l'Hindoustan, par M. de Langle." Also, Daniel's Plates, Ind. Antiq.

12—*Kedarésa*, or *Kedaranath* in the *Himalaya*. The last has been frequently visited by travellers.

In each of these temples the only image of Siva that attracted devotees was a Linga. From this circumstance, and from what has already been adduced, there can be little doubt that the religion of the Saivas, or followers of Siva (comprising a large majority of the Hindüs of Bengal), is nothing more than a regular system of Phallic idolatry.

According to his followers—and he has many even in the Deccan—*Baswá Basavá*, or *Baswapa*, the supposed founder of the faith, only *restored* the worship of *Mahadeo*, and did not invent it. This man was the son of *Madija Ráya*, a Brahman, and *Madevi* his wife, inhabitants of *Hinguleswur-pavati-Agraharam*, on the west side of *Sri Saila*, and both devout worshippers of *Siva* (*Mahadeo*).

In recompense for their piety, *Nandi*, the Sacred Bull of *Siva*, was born on earth, as their son, becoming incarnate in that animal by the command of *Siva*, who, on learning from *Nareda* the decline of his religion and the neglect with which his *Lingas* were treated, manifested himself in a miraculous manner to these two devout persons. Siva in his human form, and accompanied by

Pawati his *Sacti*, came forth from the great Sangameswarra *Linga*; thus proving that his divine essence even dwelt in these his emblems.*

From this time the adoration of the *Linga*, which had languished, again came into vogue, and, as before observed, is the principal and most venerated of all the Hindü Idols of Bengal.

But it is not only the votaries of *Siva* who adore their God under the symbolic form of the *Linga;* the Vaishnavas, or followers of Vishnu, use the same medium. They also are *Lingayetts*, one of the essential characteristics of which is wearing the Type on some part of their dress or person. The *Linga* is enclosed in a case either of silver or copper, and worn suspended from the neck, or on the arm as a bracelet (*cada*). These amulets are intended to avert the bad influence of the evil eye, and may be compared to the Fascinum of the Romans and the Jettatura of Modern Italy.†

---

* *Vide* Mackenzie's Collections, vol. ii., Halukanara MSS.

† "Sequuntur turpia atque obscena quædam fascina exaere, quae Etruscae feminæ collo suspensa gerere consueverunt, ut sibi fecunditatem a *Priapo Deo* facilius impetrarent. Ea etiam persaepe taurius capiti adiuncta sunt: quae etiam puerorum—collo tamquam remedium praebiavo appenderunt, loco *amuleti et fascini*, quod Plinius

The *Vaishnavas* are divided into many sects. They comprise the *Ghoculasthas*, the *Yonijas*, the *Ramani*, and the *Radha-ballabis.* The *Ghoculasthas* adore *Krishna*, while the *Ramani* worship *Rama*; both have again branched into three sects—one consists of the exclusive worshippers of *Krishna*, and these only are deemed true and orthodox *Vaishnávas*.

Under the name of *Gopala* (the Shepherd), *Krishna* is doubtless the same as the pastoral Apollo, who fed the herds of Admetus, surnamed Nomios by the Greeks. The destruction of Python by Apollo signifies the purification of the atmosphere by the Sun from mephitic exhalations consequent on the deluge, and *Krishna's* victory over the noxious *Kalyanaga* may be explained in the same manner. In honour of his triumph, games and sports are annually held in India [*Huli*], as the Pythic games were at stated times exhibited in Greece. Like the Pythian serpent in the temples of Apollo, *Kalya narga* enjoys also his Apotheosis in those

---

infantium custodem adpellat—[Hist. Nat. lib. xxviii. civ.]—Horum plane ingens numerus tota Etruria in Museis obvius est: e quibus antiquis reliquiis, summam pudendamque fuisse veterum Etrusorum superstitionem, probe dignoscere licet."—*Museum Etruscum exhibens insignia, &c., by Antonio Francisco Gorius*, vol. ii., p. 141, A.D. 144.

dedicated to the worship of *Krishna.* Nor are arguments wanted towards identifying Serpentarius, on our sphere, with his formidable foe, and the theatre of the warfare the river *Yamuna,* with the Vîa Lactea. Apollo and *Krishna* are both said to be inventors of the flute, one was disappointed by Daphne, who was turned into the Laurus, hence sacred to Apollo. Krishna's coy nymph was transformed into the *Tulasi,* alike sacred to him.

As *Parameswarra, Krishna* is represented of a black or dark blue colour. Now the *Tulasi* is the black Ocymun, and all animals or vegetables of a black or blue colour are sacred to him. His *Linga* also is always either black or dark blue, and may thus be distinguished from that of *Siva,* which is generally white.

This divinity, as *Parameswarra* is *Jagan'-nauth* (*Juggernaut*), or "Lord of the Universe," and it was under the wheels of his sacred car that so many misguided beings annually immolated themselves.

Krishna, from his known amorous propensities, is a peculiar favourite with the Hindü women; to which M. de Langle makes the following naïve allusion, in his description of the character of this divinity: "Au reste," he says, "on ne peut douter de son extrême penchant pour le beau sexe; car, outre huit femmes, parmi lesquelles la favorite nominée *Râdhá* est célébre par ses graces et par sa beauté, il eut 16 mille concubines trouvées toutes vierges dans le palais de *Bhoum,* demon *(âzoura)* à cinq têtes, qu'il tua à cause de ses innoubrable forfaits. Suivant quelques theologiens Hindous, *Radha,* est une incarnation de *Lakchmi* femme de *Vichnon,* incarné lui-même sous le nom de *Krishna."* *

To return, however, to the *Vaishnavas.* Another of their sects adore *Krishna* and his mistress *Radha* united. These are the *Lingionijas,* whose worship is perhaps the most free of all the *Pujas.* A third, the *Radha-ballubhis,* dedicate their offerings to *Radha* † only. The followers of these last-

---

* Monumens Ancien et Moderne de l'Hindoustan.

† *Radha, Radhica,* or *Rukmeni,* the favorite *Mistress* of Krishna, was one of the nine *Gopia* (Shepherdesses or Milkmaids), the inseparable companions of this Deity. She is an *Avata,* or incarnation of *Laksmi* or *Camala,* the spouse of Vishnu, the universal mother of Nature, and the impersonation of female beauty. She is the type of religion and spiritual love to the deity. Her characteristics are set forth in the *Gita Govisida* and *Gita Radhica Krishna,* the latter Poem bearing a most striking resemblance to the Canticles.

The loves of *Krishna* and *Radha,* which, in the writings of the Hindüs are constantly adverted to, are said to mean, in their emblematical theology, the reciprocal attraction

mentioned sects have adopted the singular practice of presenting to a naked girl the oblation intended for the Goddess, constituting her the living impersonation of *Radha.* But when a female is not to be obtained for this purpose, the votive offerings are made to an image of the Yoni, or emblem of the feminine POWER. These wor-

---

between the divine goodness and the human soul; and are told at large in the tenth book of the *Bhágavat.* In like manner is the *Bhágavat Géeta* regarded by the Brahmins, though it apparently consists of a dialogue between *Krishna* and his follower *Arjün.* We are informed that in this instance *Krishna* is to be regarded as the Supreme Being, *Arjün* as the human soul. This mysticism abounds in all their writings, but is not peculiar to the Hindüs. It is questionable whether any of their sacred writings contain one-half of the mysticism to be found in the Apocalypse of St. John.

"The separate Sects or religious systems that we find among Hindüs should never be confounded. The creed that honours Vishnu-Krishna as the Beneficent Power is quite separate from the demon worship in which Siva-Mahadeva is adored: and beyond this is the Tantra system of Magic and the destroying Powers. Rukmeni is the *wife*, not mistress, of Krishna. The wedding is described in the *Bhágavat*, which is a canonical scripture. In a later age Radha, the *mistress*, not wife of Krishna, is the heroine of a heretical work, the *Dévi Bhágavat*, or Tale of the good Goddess: and she is declared to be nature, the mother of all beings. The naked worship is quite separate, and appertains to the Tantrica or Black Magic. The Brahma Vaivartta Puran, the Kalica Puran, and some others are disowned by the orthodox Hindüs, as works of authority, who pin their faith on the *Bhárrata*, *Bhágavata*, and *Rámáyan.* All the other Puranas are rejected."

shippers are called *Yonijas*, in contradistinction to the *Lingayats*, or adorers of the *Krishna (Vishnu) Linga*.

As the *Saivas* are all worshippers of Siva and *Bowance* (Pavati) conjointly, so the Vaishnavas also offer up their prayers to *Laksmi-Nayarana*. The exclusive adorers of this Goddess are the *Sactas*.

The cast mark of the *Saivas* and *Sactas* consists of three horizontal lines on the forehead,* with ashes obtained, if possible,

---

*The question of Sectarian Marks seems to have engaged the attention of Maurice. He says, "There was another remarkable symbol of Taut, or Mercury, prevalent in Egypt as well as in India. It was the letter T, or in other words the cross, or *Crux Hermis*, in which form we find many of the more ancient Pagodas of India, as Benares and Mattra, erected; and many of the old Egyptian statues, as is well known to antiquaries, are represented bearing this symbol in their hand or on their breasts. D'Hancarville, and the generality of mythologists, explain this symbol as referring to the *gross physical worship* to which the ancients were so greatly addicted, and as an emblem of Jupiter *Generator* (or Priapus), or the deity in his creative capacity, in Ancient Egypt and India, and which Mr. Bruce frequently met with in his travels through the Higher Egypt and Abyssinia. I have elsewhere observed the very singular manner after which the Latin *Vulgate*, and, according to Louth, probably the ancient copies of the Septuagint, have rendered the original of that passage in Ezekiel ix. 4, "*I will set a mark upon their forehead;*" rendering it in their version, "I will mark them on the forehead with the letter *Tau;*" which affords room to suppose it was a symbol of a more sacred (phallic ?) import than is generally imagined," &c.—*Maurice, Ind. Antiq.*, pp. 44, 45, Lond., 1801.

from the hearth, on which a consecrated firé is perpetually maintained. The adoration of the *Sacti* * is quite in accordance with the spirit of the mythological system of the Hindüs. It has been computed that of the Hindüs in Bengal, at least *three-fourths are Sactas,* of the remaining fourth, three parts are *Vaishnavas,* and one *Saivas.*

Independently of the homage paid to the principal Deities, there are a great variety of inferior beings, *Dewtas,* and demi-gods of a malevolent character and formidable aspect, who receive the worship of the multitude. The bride of *Siva,* however, in one or other of her many and varied forms, †

---

* *Sactya Rites among Mussulmans.*

According to Buckingham, "Between Zohaub and Kermanshah there are a people called Nessereah, who, like those of the same name in Syria, pay divine honours to the Pudendum Muliebre, and hold feasts resembling ancient mysteries of Venus."

† In alluding to *Bhavani (Pavati)* as distinguished by a variety of names implying Nature, and among others using that of *Shacti* (a word that is usually and in this treatise called *Sacti*), Paolino in his Voyages, p. 327, gives an account of the Magna Mater of the Hindüs. "She changes," he says, "and transforms herself into a thousand shapes, and appears sometimes as a man and sometimes as a woman. Her votaries paint the *Medhra*" (in Bengal called *yoni*), "which is represented by two side strokes, and a red one in the middle" (on the forehead). "This mark represents the womb of *Bhavani,*" in its conventional form. —*Paolino's Voyage to Malabar.*

is by far the most popular goddess in Bengal and along the Ganges.

The worship of the female generative principle, as distinct from the Divinity, appears to have originated in the literal interpretation of the metaphorical language of the *Vedhas*, in which *Will, or purpose to Create* the Universe, is represented as originating from the Creator and co-existent with him as his bride, and part of himself. We read in the *Rig-Veda* the following—"That divine spirit breathed without afflation, single, with (*Swadha*) her who is sustained within him, other than her nothing existed." Again, "First, desire was formed in his mind, and desire became the original productive seed."* The *Sáma-Veda* also, speaking of the divine cause of creation, says, "He felt not joy, being alone. He wished for another, and instantly the desire was gratified. He caused his body to part in twain, and thus became male and female. They united, and human beings were produced.†

Prakriti,‡ the mother of gods and men,

---

* As. Res., viii. 393.

† Idem, viii., 426.

‡ *Prakriti* is inherent *Maya*, because she beguiles all beings."—As. Res., xvii.

one with matter, the source of error, is identified with *Maya* or delusion,* and co-existent with the Omnipotent, and his *Sacti*, his personified energy, his bride. According to Wilson, "these mythological fancies have principally been disseminated by the *Puranas*, and were unknown anterior to those writings" The whole subject is given *in extenso* in the *Brahma-Vaivaartta Puran* (a Purana which is not considered orthodox), under the head of *Prakrita Khanda*, in which the legends having reference to the modifications of the female principle are narrated. It is further stated in this *Puran*, that *Brahma*, having determined to create the universe, became androgynous, male and female; the right half having the sex and form of a man; the left, that of a woman. In his images he is sometimes thus represented, and is then termed Ardnari. "This is *Prakriti* of one nature with *Brahm*; illusion, eternal, as the soul so is its active

---

* On the base of Minerva's statue at Sais, whom the Egyptians regarded to be the same as Isis, a goddess who bears so striking an analogy to the Hindü *Prakriti* or nature, there was this inscription: "*I am everything that has been, that is, and that shall be: nor has any mortal ever yet been able to discover what is under my veil.*"—Plutar. de Iside et Osiride, s. ix.

energy, as the faculty of burning is in fire."*

In another passage of the *Sama Vedha* it is said that *Krishna*, being alone invested with the divine nature, began to create all things by his own will, which became manifest in Mula-Prakriti.

Wilson asserted † that "Krishna is undoubtedly a very modern intruder into the Hindü Pantheon." In what sense the term "modern" is here used is impossible now to determine, but the fact of Megasthenes ‡ having visited a temple of this divinity, whom he calls Hercules, at Mathura on the Jumna, the Matura Deorum of Ptolemy, sufficiently proves that the worship of this Divinity was instituted many years antecedent to the Christian æra. It is therefore presumed that Wilson spoke in the comparative degree, and intended to imply that, as compared with other portions of the Ritual, the Vedas for example, the deifica-

---

* Thus in the *Kuma-Puran*, c. xii., we read, "His energy, being the universal form of all the world, is *Maya*, for so does the Lord, the best of males, and endowed with illusion cause it to revolve. That *Sacti* of which the essence is illusion is omniform and eternal, and constantly displays the universal shape of *Mahesa*."

† As. Res., vol. xvii. 214—220.

‡ Vide Arrian Ind. Hist., c. viii., also Strabo.

tion of *Krishna* is modern. However that may be, a worship which, like that of *Krishna*, has existed for two thousand years, may be fairly regarded as part of their religious system.

Although the adoration of the *Sacti* is authorized by some of the Puranas, the rites and formulæ are more clearly set forth in a voluminous collection of books called *Tantras*. These writings convey their meaning in the similitude of dialogue between Uma (or *Siva*) and *Pavati*.

The followers of the *Tantras* profess to consider them as a fifth *Vedh*, and attribute to them equal antiquity and superior authority.* The observances they prescribe have in Bengal almost superseded the original Ritual, but the question of their date is involved in considerable obscurity. From the practices described in some of the *Puranas*, particularly that of the *Diksha*, or rite of initiation, from the *Agni Purán*,

---

* Thus in the Siva *Tantra*, Siva is made to say, "The five scriptures issued from my five mouths, and were the East, West, South, North, and Upper: these five are known as the paths to final liberation. There are many Scriptures, but none are equal to the Upper Scripture." *Kulluka Bhatta*, commentating on the first verse of the 2nd ch. Menu, says, "The *Scruti* is twofold, *Vaidika* and *Tantrika*, that is *Tantra*."

from the specification of formulæ, comprising the mystical monosyllables of the *Tantras*, in that and other similar compilations; and from the citation of some of them by name in different *puranas*, we must conclude that some of the *Tantras* are prior to those authorities.

The *Tantras* are too numerous to specify them further, but the curious reader will find them under the heads of *Syama Rahasya*, *Anandra*, *Rudra*, *Yamala*, *Mandra*, *Mahodahi*, *Sareda*, *Tilika*, and *Kalika-Tantras*.*

Although any of the goddesses may be objects of the *Sacta* worship, and the term *Sacti* comprehends them all, yet the homage of the *Sactas* is almost restricted, in Bengal, to the consort of Siva. The *Varnis*, or *Vamacharis*, worship *Devi* as well as all goddesses. Their worship is derived from a portion of the *Tantras*.

According to the immediate object of the worshipper is the particular form of worship; but all the forms require the use of some or all of the five *Makaras* †—*Mánsa*, *Matsya*,

---

* Vide the Sanscrit copies of the Tantras in the British and Indian Museums.

† They are enumerated in the *Syáma Rahasya*. "*Mudra* and *Maithuna* are the five-fold *Makára* which takes away all sin."

Madya, Maithuna, and *Mudra*—that is, flesh, fish, wine, women, and certain mystical gesticulations with the fingers. Suitable *muntrus,* or incantations, are also indispensable, according to the end proposed, consisting of various unmeaning monosyllabic combinations of letters, of great imaginary efficacy.*

When the object of worship is to acquire an interview with, and control over, impure spirits, a dead body is necessary. The adept is also to be alone, at midnight, in a cemetery or place where bodies are burnt. Seated on the corpse, he is to perform the usual offerings, and if he do so without fear or disgust, the *Dhutas,* the *Yoginis,* and other male and female demons become his slaves.

In this and many of the observances practised, solitude is enjoined, but all the principal ceremonies comprehend the worship of *Sacti,* or POWER, and require, for that purpose, the presence of a young and beautiful girl, as the living representative of the goddess.† This worship is mostly cele-

* "It is the combination of H and S called *Prásáda Mantra,* and described in the *Kulárnava.*"—Wilson, As. Res.

† The female thus worshipped is ever after denominated Yogini, *i.e.,* "attached." This Sanscrit word is in the

brated in a mixed society ; the men of which represent *Bhairavas*, or *Viras*, and the women, *Bhanravis* and *Nayikas*. The Sacti is personified by a naked girl, to whom meat and wine are offered, and then distributed among the assistants. Here follows the chanting of the *Muntrus* and sacred texts, and the performance of the *Mudra*, or gesticulations with the fingers. The whole terminates with orgies amongst the votaries of a very licentious description.* This ceremony is entitled the SRI CHAKRA, or PURNABISHEKA, THE RING or full Initiation.†

---

dialects pronounced Jogi or Zogee, and is equivalent to a secular nun, as these women are subsequently supported by alms. The word from custom has become equivalent with *Sena*, and thus is exactly the same as *Duti* or Dutica, (*doo-ty-car*). The books of morality direct a faithful wife to shun the society of Yogini, or females who have been adored as Sacti.

The Sacti system bears a striking affinity with Epicureanism. It teaches Materialism and the Atomic system of chance. (Compare the *Ananda Tantram*, c. xvii. with *Lucretius*, lib. iii.)

The worship of women and the *Sacta h'oma vidhi* are grounded on passages in the Veda which orthodox Brahmins regard as of doubtful authority. (Vide Rig Vedam, Bk. ii. c. viii. sections 13, 14, 2nd attham, 8th pannam, ricks B. 14, which contain the *Sucla Homa Mantram*, &c.)

* Wilson, on Hin. Sects, vol. xvii., As Res.

† Ward, on the Vaisnavis, p. 309.

The leading rites of the *Sakti Sodhana* are described in the *Devi Radhasya*, a section of the *Rudra Yámala*. It

This method of adoring the Sacti is unquestionably acknowledged by the texts regarded by the Vanis as authorities for the impurities practised.

The members of the sect are sworn to secrecy, and will not therefore acknowledge any participation in Sacta-Puja. Some years ago, however, they began to throw off this reserve, and at the present day they trouble themselves very little to disguise their initiation into its mysteries, but they do not divulge in what those mysteries consist.

The Culanava has the following and other similar passages: the Tantras abound with them:

" Many false pretenders to knowledge,

---

is therein stated that the object of worship should be either "A dancing girl, a female devotee, a courtesan, *Dhobee* woman, a barber's wife, a female of the Brahminical or Sudra tribe, a flower girl, or a milk-maid. Appropriate *muntrus* are to be used. She is to be placed naked, but richly ornamented with jewels and flowers, on the left of a circle described for the purpose, with various *muntrus* and gesticulations, and it is to be rendered pure by the repetition of different formulas, being finally sprinkled over *with wine* by the peculiar *mantra*.

"The *Sacti* is now purified, but if not previously initiated, she is to be further made an adept by the communication of the Radical *Mantra* whispered thrice in her ear, when the object of the ceremony is complete. The finale is what might be anticipated, but accompanied throughout by *muntrus*, and forms of meditation very foreign to the scene."—Wilson, As. Res., vol. xvii. 225, on Hin. Sects.

and who have not been duly initiated, pretend to practise the Caula rites; but if perfection be attained by drinking wine, then every drunkard is a saint; if virtue consists in eating flesh, then every carnivorous animal in the world is virtuous; if eternal happiness be derived from the union of the sexes, then all beings will be entitled to it. A follower of the Cula doctrine is blameless in my sight if he reproves those of other creeds who quit their established observances. Those of other sects who use the articles of the Caula worship shall be condemned to a metempsychosis during as many years as there are hairs of the body."

The Kauchilüas are another branch of the Sactas sect; their worship much resembles that of the Caulas. They are, however, distinguished by one particular rite not practised by the others, and throw into confusion all the ties of female relationship; natural restraints are wholly disregarded, and a community of women among the votaries inculcated.*

---

* This sect appears in the *Sankara Vijaya* as the *Uchchishtha Ganapati* or *Hairamba* sect, who declare that all men and all women are of one caste, and that their intercourse is free from fault."—Vide Ward's Works, vol. ii. 5, on the above subject.—*Wilson on Hin. Sects*, vol. xvii.

On the occasions of the performance of divine worship the women and girls deposit their *julies*, or bodices, in a box in charge of the *Gurü*, or priest. At the close of the rites, the male worshippers take each a *julie* from the box, and the female to whom it belongs, even were she his sister, becomes his partner for the evening in these lascivious orgies.*

Dancing formed an important part of the ceremonial worship of most Eastern peoples. Dancing girls were attached to the Egyptian temples and to that of the Jews. David also, we are told, "danced before the Lord with all his might." And to every temple of any importance in India we find a troup of *Nautch* or dancing girls attached.

These women are generally procured when quite young, and are early initiated into all the mysteries of their profession. They are instructed in dancing and vocal and instrumental music, their chief employment being to chant the sacred hymns, and perform nautches before the God, on the recurrence of high festivals. But this is not the only service required of them, for besides being the acknowledged mistresses of the offici-

---

* Yet these *Sacteyas* (or adorers of *Sacti*) look upon all but themselves as "*pasu jana*," mere brutes!

ating priests, it is their duty to prostitute themselves in the courts of the temple to all comers, and thus raise funds for the enrichment of the place of worship to which they belong.

Being always women of considerable personal attractions, which are heightened by all the seductions of dress, jewels, accomplishments and art, they frequently receive large sums in return for the favours they grant, and fifty, one hundred, and even two hundred rupees have been known to be paid to these syrens in one night. Nor is this very much to be wondered at, as they comprise among their number, perhaps, some of the loveliest women in the world.

It has been said already that among the classes from which a medium for *Sacti* is selected, is the courtesan and dancing-girl grade; they are indeed more frequently chosen for this honour than the others before enumerated. A *Nautch* woman esteems it a peculiar privilege to become the *Radha Dea* on such occasions. It is an office indeed which these adepts are, on every account, better calculated to fulfil with satisfaction to the sect of Sacteyas who require their aid, than a more innocent and unsophisticated girl.

The worship of *Sacti* (as already observed)

is the adoration of POWER,* which the Hindūś typify by the *Yoni,* or womb, the *Argha* or *Vulva,* and by the leaves and flowers of certain plants thought to resemble it. Thus in the *Anandra Tantram,* c. vi., verse 13, we find an allusion to the *Aswattha,* or sacred fig-tree (the leaf of which is in the shape of a heart, and much resembles the conventional form of the *Yoni,* to which it is compared).

> "*Aswattha patra sadrusam Yoniáciáram cha bhàjànam.*
> *Támra, rúpya, suvaruaistu rachitam tal prasasyate.*"

In *Ananda Tantram,* cap. vii. 148, and other passages, reference is made to *Bhagamala.* She appears to be the goddess who presides over the *pudendum muliebre,* i.e., the deified *Vulva;* and the *Sacti* is thus personified.

In the mental adoration of Sacti a diagram is framed, and the figure imagined to be seen inside the *Vulva.* This is the *Adhamukham,* or lower face, i.e., the *Yoni,*

---

*In Egypt we learn that *Typho* sometimes bore the name *Seth,* "by which they mean the *Tyrannical* and *overbearing* POWER, or, as the word frequently signifies, the POWER that overturns all things, and that overleaps all bounds."—Plutar. de Iside et Osirides, xxxvi.

wherein the worshipper is to imagine (*mantapam*) a chapel to be erected.*

All the forms of *Sacti Puja* require the use of some or all of the five—*Makaras*† *Mansa*, *Matsya*, *Madya*, *Maithuna*, and *Mudra*—that is, flesh, fish, wine, women, and certain mystical twistings or gesticulations with the fingers.

Such are some of the peculiar features of the worship of POWER (or Gnosticism),‡ and which, combined with the Linga Puja (or adoration of Phallus), constitutes at the present day one of the most popular dogmas of the Hindüs.

---

* Amanda Tantram.

† They are enumerated in the *Syama Rahasya*. "*Mudra* and Maithuna are the five-fold *Makára*, which takes away all sin."

‡ Simon Magus is supposed to be the founder of Western Gnosticism, he it was who corrupted the Nicolaitanes [*vide* Apocalypse, ii. 6, 15]. They held sensual pleasure to be the true creed.

In the Foreign Quarterly Review, p. 159, 580, the following passage occurs:—"The grand object of the magic of the Christians in the middle ages was to obtain the command over the services of demons: such were the pursuits of witches. But these were always looked upon as criminal. The belief that men possess the power to control spirits was not peculiar to the Gnostick Christians. The liturgies of the Roman and Greek churches contain several rules on these subjects."

The Memoirs of Scipio di Ricci, of Pistoja, reveal some remarkable facts, plainly demonstrating that Sacteya ideas had found their way into the monasteries and convents of Italy in the latter part of the last century.

Demand Any Rare Book at:

www.facsimilepublisher.com

if not available, give information,
our team will search and update you.

Promote Knowledge:

If you have any rare book
which is not available at
www.facsimilepublisher.com,
offer it to other readers so that others can also be
benefitted with your cooperation.
The book will be printed with your courtesy.

Print & Publish:

If you wish to get your book printed or published,
we have the service for you.

Customization on Demand:

We offer customization of books
as per the demand of the customer.

Published by

Facsimile Publisher
Ashok Vihar, Delhi-110052 (India)
Website: www.facsimilepublisher.com

Distributed by

Gyan Books Pvt. Ltd.
5, Ansari Road, Daryaganj, New Delhi-110002 (India)
E-mail: books@gyanbooks.com, Website: www.gyanbooks.com

2 222000 000820